He Told Me

Hearing God's Voice & Hoping in His Promises

KAROLYNE ROBERTS

Copyright ©

He Told Me: Hearing God's Voice & Hoping in His Promises

ISBN: 9781694891617

© 2019 by Karolyne Roberts. All rights reserved.

No portion of this book may be reproduced, stored in a retrieval system, or transmitted in any form or by any means except for brief quotations in printed reviews without the prior written permission of Karolyne Roberts.

Requests should be addressed to Karolyne Roberts at info@KarolyneRoberts.com

For information on bulk orders please contact Luminous Publishing at info@luminouspublishing.org

Printed in the United States of America.

Scripture quotations are taken from the Holy Bible, King James Version, New King James Version, New Living Translation, and New International Version. Used by permission of Tyndale House Publishers, Inc. Carol Stream, Illinois 60188. All rights reserved.

Publisher: Luminous Publishing

Table of Contents

Part 1: God Speaks in Many Ways 1

   Introduction 2

   CHAPTER 1: Logos 3

   CHAPTER 2: Rhema 10

   CHAPTER 3: Called by God 17

   CHAPTER 4: An Example of You 24

Part 2: Revelatory Gifts of the Spirit 30

   Introduction 31

   CHAPTER 5: Prophetically Speaking 33

   CHAPTER 6: Tongues & Interpretation 41

   CHAPTER 7: Word of Knowledge 48

   CHAPTER 8: Word of Wisdom 51

   CHAPTER 9: Visions and Dreams 58

   CHAPTER 10: Why Is God Silent? 64

Part 1

God Speaks in Many Ways

Introduction

In part one of this book, you will learn of the different ways God speaks to every believer. All children of God have the ability to hear Him in the following ways:

- We understand the tangible Word of God through *logos*
- We hear divine utterances from God as *rhema*
- We receive an invitation from God in our *calling*
- We learn from life experiences and *examples*

As you read, you will learn how to understand the *logos* word, hear the *rhema* word, respond to the calling of God, and learn from the examples God uses in our everyday lives. My prayer is that this book will be the start of a transformative journey in your relationship with God and your ability to hear His voice.

The two Greek words, *logos* and *rhema* are very important when it comes to hearing from God. *Logos* is God's constant written word from the Bible. *Rhema* is an instant personal word we receive from God. The more you have *Logos* within you, the greater your capacity to receive a *Rhema* word.

CHAPTER 1

Logos

People say, "Well, God doesn't speak to me. He just doesn't!" But God is always speaking. He is an eternal God and the Bible is described as His eternal Word! "Heaven and Earth will pass away but my words will never pass away" (Matthew 24:35). God's Word will never pass away because it is eternal. Meaning, God is speaking now. He spoke in the past, and He's going to be speaking tomorrow. He is always speaking. But are you listening? Are you reading His Word? Are you available to listen to the truth He sends forth? Or do you have itchy ears? Do you pick and choose from His Word and all these different sources, people on social media, and whatever your flesh wants to hear?

God speaks directly from the written Word or in accordance with the Bible, which is known as Logos. When God speaks, you will have peace about it. When the Enemy speaks it's contrary to God's Word or it's a twisted version of it. If you don't know God's Word, how will you decipher whether or not what you're hearing is twisted? That takes attention to detail, true knowledge, and a holistic understanding of God and

Scripture. The Enemy will cut and paste Scripture and leave parts of it out. You need to know God's Word thoroughly, not just a few popular Bible verses. Knowing the God of the Word and having a personal relationship with Him is also crucial.

Your thoughts shouldn't matter because you can think carnally today (in the flesh) but spiritually tomorrow. So if you're in the flesh today, your thoughts will be in accordance with what the Enemy is saying. If you're in the Spirit tomorrow, your thoughts will be in line with what God is saying. Discerning what you are hearing is not as complicated as, "Is it me, God or the Devil?" It's as simple as, "Is this contrary to God's Word or not?" You should be concerned with what God is saying. Who cares what you're saying? Or why care what the Devil is saying?

What is God saying? When you find that out, when you find that His Word lines up, pray and go forth with the leading of the Holy Spirit. We will know it's Him if we are actually spending time with Him.

We need to spend time with God's Word to the point where we are meditating on it and carrying it inside of us. Are you simply rushing your Bible study or devotional time so you can mark it off your list? Do you desire the false validation that comes after you've accomplished another religious work? Or are you actually ingesting and digesting every single part of God's Word? You may be reading passages with some great revelation but if you are not digesting God's Word the right way, you won't hear what He is trying to say to you. Take your time!

The Bible is often referred to as food. Jesus is God's Word Himself, the Bread of Life. "Jesus answered, "It is written: 'Man shall not live on bread alone, but on every word that comes from the mouth of God" (Matthew 4:4). We are to live on God's Word. It is our sustenance and spiritual food. In the same way the lack of natural food makes our physical bodies weak and hard to function, when we fail to eat our spiritual food, parts of our spiritual bodies such as our spiritual ears become weak and dysfunctional as well. We can't hear God clearly when we are not feasting on His Word. Neglecting to feed on the Word starves our spiritual organs, especially the eyes and ears.

Not only is it essential to read God's Word, but we must also learn to meditate on it. In other words, we should take our time and deeply focus our minds on Scripture. According to preciousnutrituon.com, "The benefits of slow eating include better digestion, better hydration, easier weight loss or maintenance, and greater satisfaction with our meals." I believe this concept applies spiritually as well. When we slowly take in God's Word and take our time to meditate on what we are reading, we digest it better. We get more satisfaction out of our Bible reading experience. God's Word is hidden in our hearts, and we are carrying it with us wherever we go. "I have hidden your word in my heart, that I might not sin against you" (Psalm 119:11).

Meditating on God's Word and slowly digesting it causes it to take root as a seed and grow into a beautiful harvest of spiritual fruit. When we take our time, we have a better understanding of what God is saying to us. However, when we don't reverence God's Word in this way, the Enemy comes to steal the seed and hinder our revelation of it. Believe it or not, the way you receive and digest God's Word is important; it makes a big difference. Your response to the Bible reflects the condition of the soil in which the seed will be planted. If you read God's Word with a hardened heart, the soil of your understanding will be dry and rough. It will be very difficult to penetrate your heart with good seed and will require cleansing water for true growth.

Let's read Matthew 13:3-9 for a greater example:

> He told many stories in the form of parables, such as this one: "Listen! A farmer went out to plant some seeds. As he scattered them across his field, some seeds fell on a footpath, and the birds came and ate them. Other seeds fell on shallow soil with underlying rock. The seeds sprouted quickly because the soil was shallow. But the plants soon wilted under the hot sun, and since they didn't have deep roots, they died. Other seeds fell among thorns that grew up and choked out the tender plants. Still other seeds fell on fertile soil, and they produced a crop that was thirty, sixty, and even a hundred times as much as had been planted! Anyone with ears to hear should listen and understand.

This parable Jesus shared is about hearing God's voice. It refers to the condition of your heart and whether or not God's Word can penetrate it. So what is the condition of your heart?

Is your heart in a condition to hear God when you read His Word? Or is your heart shallow? Is your heart going to choke up the very thing God is saying to you?

I encourage you to pray every time before you open your Bible to read. Ask God to create a clean heart and renew a right spirit within you according to Psalm 51:10. Ask Him to soften your hardened heart and open your eyes to reveal what you cannot see. Your soil needs to be soft and fertile to receive the seed.

The Holy Spirit is the best teacher. He is here to lead and guide us into all truth (John 16:13). You can't read and understand God's Word with natural ears and eyes. You can only do so by spiritual means because it requires spiritual understanding.

Let's continue with Matthew 13:14-23, which reads:

> This fulfills the prophecy of Isaiah that says, 'When you hear what I say, you will not understand. When you see what I do, you will not comprehend. For the hearts of these people are hardened, and their ears cannot hear, and they have closed their eyes—so their eyes cannot see, and their ears cannot hear, and their hearts cannot understand, and they cannot turn to me and let me heal them.' "But blessed are your eyes, because they see; and your ears, because they hear. I tell you the truth, many prophets and righteous people longed to see what you see,

but they didn't see it. And they longed to hear what you hear, but they didn't hear it. "Now listen to the explanation of the parable about the farmer planting seeds: The seed that fell on the footpath represents those who hear the message about the Kingdom and don't understand it. Then the evil one comes and snatches away the seed that was planted in their hearts. The seed on the rocky soil represents those who hear the message and immediately receive it with joy. But since they don't have deep roots, they don't last long. They fall away as soon as they have problems or are persecuted for believing God's word. The seed that fell among the thorns represents those who hear God's word, but all too quickly the message is crowded out by the worries of this life and the lure of wealth, so no fruit is produced. The seed that fell on good soil represents those who truly hear and understand God's word and produce a harvest of thirty, sixty, or even a hundred times as much as had been planted!

We must take the time to meditate on God's Word and ask the Holy Spirit to help us understand it. You can't approach Scripture with natural eyes, rush through the reading, and expect to discern what it means. It doesn't work that way! With that approach, you will never hear and perceive what the Lord is trying to say to you through His Word. Hence, 1 Corinthians

2:14 says, "The natural person does not accept the things of the Spirit of God, for they are folly to him, and he is not able to understand them because they are spiritually discerned."

We must be intentional about spending time with the Lord daily. That way, we will recognize that, indeed, He is always speaking. Don't rush your quiet time or Bible reading time. Schedule your day so you have ample time to meditate and reflect on God's Word.

I like to meditate on scriptures by writing them out in my journal or jotting them down on index cards. Reading it is one thing, but writing down the entire scripture, requires your full attention. You will take your time and focus on it. You can also carry around an index card with you and meditate on a particular scripture throughout the day. I also like to go further into my study by cross-referencing different versions of the Bible. I use a Bible concordance to go deeper into my study, looking up the Greek and Hebrew definitions or finding related verses.

It is a beautiful exploration. You can never know the entire Bible because even after you have read it all, I guarantee if you read it again, you will find new, hidden gems you failed to uncover before. God's Word is exceedingly deep. It is an eternal treasure hunt where we can experience more of His truth and love. Why scratch the surface alone? Explore the Word and discover the deep seeds and nuggets of gold waiting to be found if only you would take your time and realize God is always speaking.

CHAPTER 2

Rhema

When you have a personal relationship with God, you should be able to distinguish the voice of God from the voice of the Devil or your own. In any close relationship, the people involved know each other's voices. You know the voices of your husband, wife, best friend, children, and other loved ones because you communicate with them on a daily basis. Even if you are in a crowded arena with that person, and he/she calls out to you, you will quickly recognize the voice. It's the same thing with God. Several things can be going on in our lives, and spiritually, we may be in a crowded room. Nevertheless, if we are in a personal relationship with God we should hear the still, gentle voice of the Holy Spirit speaking to us.

Many of us struggle to hear God's voice because our lives are filled with distractions and lots of noise. We spend countless hours on social media when we could be pursuing a closer relationship with God. How can you know the voice of someone you don't spend time with? To hear God speaking to you, find a quiet space to be alone with Him and pull away from the noise.

I am a mother, wife, and entrepreneur, so naturally, my life can get very noisy. It's safe to say I am pulled in many different directions. The demands are many: from my kids who want juice, snacks, to watch their favorite TV show and several other things—to having conversations with my husband about how his day was, and so forth. Even with business, my phone is always alerting me of emails and notifications I have to tend to. The busyness of life makes it difficult for me to retreat to a quiet space; something is always going on.

That is why I wake up earlier than my entire family to spend at least two hours with God in the morning. I also try to put my kids to bed early, so I can spend a minimum of an hour of quiet time with God at night. This is not a formula because everyone's situation is different. It is simply what works for me in my current season. The key is to intentionally make time to spend with God. Not just any type of time but *quiet* time.

Of course, you can spend time with God throughout the day at a coffee shop, driving the car, or walking, but is it really quiet? You may miss exactly what the Holy Spirit is trying to tell you amid all the background noise, honking, coffee machines working, etc. So I prefer to spend time with God when the world is sleeping. It's much easier to hear Him that way because when the world is quiet, the voice of the Lord can be amplified.

Don't bring your phone with you when having quiet time with God. If you do have your phone, turn it off or put it on "Do not disturb" mode. It never fails. Phones can easily interrupt your time with God. Constant alerts, phone calls, texts or notifications can shift your focus from God's presence. It is rude to pick up the phone in the middle of a conversation with God to engage with someone else. How would you like it if someone did that to you?

If you want to reap the benefits of quality time in God's presence, I urge you to get rid of your phone at all costs so the Enemy cannot tempt you. I recall a time I had my phone with me; it was on silent. I had no intention of using my phone but the Enemy lured me into the trap of distraction. He put thoughts in my mind like, "Oh, you forgot to send that email!" or "You need to open your phone and check on this right away." Listen, everything can wait! You don't need to do any of that! Let the to-do list wait an hour; it is not the end of the world.

After you have gotten into this quiet space, it's time to quiet your soul. If your thoughts are raging, but your soul is at war within you, then you're still pretty loud and will have a hard time hearing from God. I like to do two things to quiet my soul: journal and worship. This helps me to pour out my heart to God and cast my cares before Him. They help my soul to rest, so He can speak to me.

I love the verses in Matthew 11:28-30, which read, "Then Jesus said, 'Come to me, all of you who are weary and carry heavy burdens, and I will give you rest. Take my yoke upon you. Let me teach you because I am humble and gentle at heart, and you will find rest for your souls. For my yoke is easy to bear, and the burden I give you is light.'"

I journal to God everything that is on my heart—all my worries and stress. I also journal how much I love Him and take it as an opportunity to thank Him for who He is and all He has done in my life. Having a spirit of thankfulness naturally transitions you into a place of worship. Most of the time, I begin to worship from my heart. I don't use my phone or computer for worship music during quiet time because of the distractions that can pop up, especially advertisements. Sometimes I might incorporate outside music if I feel led.

Once the atmosphere is quiet and your soul is quiet before God, it's time to get your mouth quiet. Seriously, some of us get close to hearing God, but we ruin it because we talk too much. We must learn how to spend more time listening and less time talking. The beautiful thing about it is one word from God can change your entire life! What you take years to research, build, and learn, can be downloaded to you in a moment from the Holy Spirit. But even more so, man's knowledge can only get you so far. God's wisdom and supernatural insight are reserved for His children who seek His face.

"You will seek me and find me when you seek me with all your heart." - Jeremiah 29:13

I spend 5-15 minutes just lying down on my bed in complete silence. Then out of the blue, I hear His quiet, gentle voice and receive a word. I know its God. I am His sheep. Jesus is the Good Shepherd who lays down His life for the sheep (John 10:11). Apart from Him, the great Shepherd, we are lost.

Part I - God Speaks in Many Ways

If we do not know Jesus, we do not know His voice, and we will wander and afflict ourselves. We will seek another voice to follow.

"My sheep listen to my voice; I know them, and they follow me."
- John 10:27

God can speak to us and tell us what He desires. He spoke to men and women throughout the entire Bible. Actually, the Bible itself was written by men who were inspired by the Holy Spirit. Therefore, we can't grow bitter and act as if God wouldn't speak to people or share something with them about their future. Who are we to judge that? Of course, you can judge by the fruit but as long as what is being said doesn't contradict what God says in His Word, God could have very well told them something.

You may ask, "Why would God tell them that?" You judge people and conjure up reasons in your mind why God wouldn't speak to them on "that level." You may think the person isn't that great of a Christian and can't even do "this" or "that" simple thing right.

How do you know what God would do? What if God is revealing something specific to those you are judging, so they can get their lives together? Why do we constantly assume we know if God would do this or that when the Bible clearly says God works in mysterious ways? (Isaiah 45:15). It also tells us God's thoughts are above our thoughts and ways above our ways (Isaiah 55:8)

Are you that super-holy Christian who is bitter because other people are hearing from God? Are you thinking: *but God never shared anything like that with me?* You have to realize your spiritual walk and relationship with God is different from the next person. God is not going to deal with you the same way He deals with everyone else.

Just the other day, I heard God speaking to me about going to a certain place. I wanted to make sure it was Him, so I asked Him for confirmation. If God gives you instruction but you need confirmation, ask Him. He oftentimes sends it. Within a time span of 24 hours, God gave me three signs and two dreams to confirm the word He had spoken to me. I knew it was God speaking to me, not the Devil because God spoke in the form of a thought, and I responded by praying in my head. I never said anything out loud about what God was speaking. He is the only one who is omniscient, omnipresent and can read our minds. He is everywhere at the same time, and He knows the thoughts of men.

"O Lord, you have examined my heart and know everything about me. You know when I sit down or stand up. You know my thoughts even when I'm far away. You see me when I travel and when I rest at home. You know everything I do." - Psalm 139:1-3

Satan can't be everywhere at the same time. He doesn't know your thoughts. However, because he has been around for so long, and he studies the patterns of men, he can guess what you are going to do. Many times he knows what your weaknesses are, so he understands where and how to tempt you.

When you open your mouth and speak at the wrong time, Satan launches attacks against you, and you question if you really heard God.

Sometimes God will tell people the very things He told you and send them directly to you as a confirmation. But do not be deceived. Pray after every encounter you have with someone you think you're receiving confirmation from. It may not be from God. The Devil knows how believers operate. He studies us and our interactions with God, as well as one another. Hence, He may try to copy God and deceive us, making us think it is God when it is not Him at all.

If you want the Lord to give you revelations about your life—secret things—you need to keep your eyes on Him, not on others or their stories. To climb God's holy mountain, we must focus on and draw closer to Him. If you take your eyes off Him, you will fall on the way up. This is what happened when Peter began walking on the water headed toward Jesus in Matthew Chapter 14. He got distracted. He took His eyes off Jesus and in fear, focused on the wind and the waves. Consequently, he started to sink. Don't get distracted! Don't take your eyes off the Lord. Continue to seek Him in every season.

CHAPTER 3

Called by God

How do you know when God has called you to do something? How do you discover your purpose and recognize God's leading in your life? Well, in this chapter, I will talk about how you can hear God's voice and instructions concerning your destiny. This is important because knowing your purpose and doing what God has called you to do allows you to live a life that glorifies Him.

Your purpose is the reason you were created. A lot of times, we make the mistake of thinking our purpose is our occupation or title. However, the only way you can know your purpose is by going to the Creator of that purpose. God, Himself is the Creator and only He knows the reason He created you. That is why I stress the importance of having a personal and intimate relationship with God. If you're not spending time with the One who created you, how can you know your purpose?

Remember, your purpose is not your occupation or title; it is the reason you were created. Only God knows the real reason. For example, the seatbelt has many characteristics; it does many different things. It can stretch and is very flexible but was the seatbelt created to stretch? No! Even though the seatbelt stretches and is flexible, it wasn't created with that purpose in mind. Rather, its ultimate purpose is to protect lives.

The point is you may have different gifts, characteristics, and talents but those things are not your purpose. They may be qualities and personality traits God placed inside you but that doesn't always mean it is your specific purpose.

Even though I'm a writer, and people can describe me as one or ascribe that title to me, being a writer is not my purpose. Sharing the gospel is. I know if I write a book that has nothing to do with sharing the gospel and leading people to Christ, I'm not operating in my purpose but my gifting. You must know why God created you.

The question of purpose is, "Why am I here?" You may have different gifts, talents, and jobs or you may find yourself in different seasons or places in life but your purpose is foundational. When you're flowing in your natural abilities, gifts, and talents, go back to the core of everything and ask yourself, why am I doing this? This may help give you and inclination of your purpose.

Ask yourself, why am I motivated to do this? What is my motivation? What inside of me makes me want to do it? What is my why? What is the reason? Everyone has a purpose to glorify God. Whatever we do, we should glorify God. However, not everyone's purpose is the same.

What is that specific thing that drives you? Everyone's why is different. I know my why is that I don't want people to go to hell; I want people to know the truth and be saved. That drives everything I do. So you have to find your why, which is the core of your purpose. No matter what you're doing, it's going to come back to, "Why am I doing this?"

Purpose and calling are two different things. Remember, your purpose is foundational. God created you with a purpose from the beginning of the earth. It is the foundation; your purpose is set before you even start living. God knew Jeremiah's purpose before he was even born. Jeremiah 1:5 says, "Before I formed you in the womb I knew you; Before you were born I sanctified you; I ordained you a prophet to the nations."

Now, let's talk about your calling. A calling usually takes place during your lifetime, even though God knows what He will call you to do in advance. God gives you an invitation. He is calling you. He is reaching out to you. He instructs you to do something specific. This could take place as a specific event—maybe through a dream or you may hear His voice telling you to do something. Perhaps God's calling might have been confirmed over a period of time through different people. The way and experience of being called are different for everyone. But God will always anoint you for what He has called you to do. He will give you the ability to carry it out and perform it through His supernatural power.

Your calling can change in different seasons. It is a way to carry out your purpose. I talked about how writing is one of my gifts; writing is also one of my callings. I know it's a calling because God literally told me: "I want you to write a book." It's almost as if He called me on the phone, "Karolyne, I want you to write a book." Not literally, but you should know God is leading you if you feel that nudge of the Holy Spirit, and you receive confirmation.

If God has spoken a specific assignment on your life and told you to do a particular task then that's what He has called you to do. He has commissioned you to a specific position. That is a calling through which you are going to carry out your purpose. So when you think of calling, imagine God is calling you on the phone. What is that thing the Holy Spirit is nudging you to do? He is saying, "I want you to do this, okay."

You are called to do something. You are not called to do your purpose because your purpose is already inside of you. It is not something you do. Rather, it is something you know. It is your motivation or the reason you were created. Your calling is something you do because God has called you to do it. Maybe your purpose is to inspire people to eat healthier and treat their bodies like the temple of God. Perhaps God put you here to be an agent of change in the health industry. God can use different callings in your life at different seasons, so you can fulfill your purpose through different callings. You may be called to write a book or blog about health or be a doctor.

Being a doctor may be what you are called to do but that may not necessarily be your purpose. Your purpose is why did God create me to be a doctor? Why am I a doctor? What am I supposed to do as a doctor? It may be as simple as coming up with a new idea, cure for a disease or giving people hope in the hospital. Everyone has a different purpose and specific reason for being here, but we can all share our callings. We're all here for a unique purpose.

No one can do what you were specifically designed to do. That's why God made us all unique. We all have different fingerprints. It is essential to do what we are called to do and live out our purpose because the world needs it. No one else can touch the world like you were specifically designed to.

Just because you don't know your purpose does not mean you don't have a purpose. It also does not mean you're outside of God's will. I was walking in my purpose before I knew what my purpose was. As long as you're being obedient to what God wants you to do in this season, right now, you're operating in purpose. You may not know what it is yet, but it's just a matter of time. Be obedient where you are today, even if you are one of those who say, "I'm over 30, but I don't know my purpose."

If you have a relationship with God and you're where He wants you to be, you're in your purpose; you're living out your purpose. You may not know it but that job you're in right now is where you are living your purpose out. You may not know why you're there but if God told you to be at that job, there is a purpose for being there. What did God tell you to do? God is preparing you; He's teaching you the fruit of the Spirit (patience, kindness, love, self-control, etc.) for the next season He's calling you to.

I went through many seasons in life where I just did not get it. I was asking, "Why the heck am I here right now, God? What are you doing? Why are you doing this? I just want to know my purpose and I want to live it out. I want to walk in my purpose."

Now that I know my purpose, I can look back and say, "Oh, that's what I was doing in that season. Oh, that's what I was learning at that place. Oh, that's why I had to go through that. I had to heal through that. God, I see how You were putting it together. I see how You were working things out for my good."

All the pieces of the puzzle are going to come together, and it will make sense in due season.

"And we know that in all things God work for the good of those who love Him, who have been called according to His purpose."
- Romans 8:28

    That's what "If you love God, you will obey His commands" means because that's what the Bible says. If you obey His commands, it means you are called according to His purpose. Do what God has called you to do, so you can live out your purpose. In doing so, all things will work out for your good, no matter what season you are in. Again, what has God called you to do?
    Be content in the season you're in and know it's going to work out for your good; you are living out your purpose. Don't compare your journey to others because they appear to be walking out their purpose. No, if you're walking in obedience every day, you will wake up in the morning and give God your "yes." That yes may mean being a stay-at-home mom. God may say, "I want you to take care of your kids in this season." That's your opportunity to say yes. As simple as that may seem, you are walking in your purpose. You don't need to start a business. You don't have to go out and start a ministry. You don't have to do something big for the world to see you're walking out your purpose. You don't need the acclaim of men. You don't need an award. You don't need to get a title. You do not need any of these things to feel you're walking in your purpose.

As I said before, your relationship with the Creator and your obedience to Him keeps you walking in your purpose. It's just a matter of time before He reveals it to you in the right season.

If God had told me my purpose in middle or high school, I wouldn't be ready because I was already running away from Him. At that time, I had no idea what my purpose was, and I wasn't ready to hear it. I couldn't even handle the simple instructions. Maybe God can't trust you to tell you your purpose because you're going to run away from Him. You still find it difficult to handle the simple instructions. What has God told you to do?

CHAPTER 4

An Example of You

When God tells you to do something that does not make sense to everyone else, do it anyway. He may just be trying to make an example of you so do it out of obedience. One thing I realized about hearing God's voice is that He speaks to us in many different ways. He doesn't always speak audibly; actually, He rarely speaks to us that way. But sometimes God uses the lives of those around us or our experiences as examples to teach us His will.

The parables Jesus told are perfect examples of this. When Jesus walked the earth, He seldom taught or preached directly in plain scripture or spiritual revelation. Jesus often used examples of everyday life to prove a point or demonstrate what He was saying. He taught the people with parables.

According to Biblehub.com, the definition of a parable is: metaphorically, a comparing, comparison of one thing with another, likeness, similitude: universally, *an example* by which a doctrine or precept is illustrated, a thing serving as a figure of something else.

Clearly, a parable is an example of God speaking. In one instance, when Jesus was sharing the parable of the sower, His disciples asked Him why He spoke as He did. Jesus responded in Matthew 13:13, "This is why I speak to them in parables: 'Though seeing, they do not see;   though hearing, they do not hear or understand.'"

The preceding verse gives a great revelation about hearing God's voice. It is not simply God's desire for you to hear what He is saying, but to also *understand* what He means. Therefore, He gives us examples. Many of us have heard God's word many times. Or maybe the Lord has spoken to you concerning a certain situation on several occasions. Yet, you complain and say, "Why isn't God speaking to me?" It is not that God isn't speaking to you. It is not that you don't hear. It is simply that you don't understand. We must get understanding. In fact, we are commanded to do so.

"Wisdom is the principal thing; Therefore get wisdom. And in all your getting, get understanding." - Proverbs 4:7

Sometimes what God tells you to do may sound crazy or socially unacceptable. That's exactly what I felt when He told me to leave university during my last semester, a few months before graduation. I have learned the importance of asking God for wisdom and understanding in these moments because such situations are peculiar. Don't add your craziness to it by making hasty, foolish decisions. You can carry out the peculiar instructions God gives you in a way that brings Him glory at the end of the day.

Part I - God Speaks in Many Ways

"If you need wisdom, ask our generous God, and he will give it to you. He will not rebuke you for asking."
- James 1:5

God wanted to use my situation as an opportunity to speak to others. He wanted to use me as an example to show people you don't necessarily need a degree to be successful. All you need is to be obedient to the Lord. I started a successful business and became a best-selling author without officially getting my creative writing degree. After having two kids and becoming a wife, God sent me back to school to show that anything is possible with Him.

I completed university despite all my responsibilities as a wife, mother, entrepreneur, and minister. I graduated 9 years from the first time I stepped foot on my college campus, but it was all in God's perfect timing. He got the glory at the end of the day. What is God saying to you? Are you willing to let Him use you for His glory? Are you willing to be obedient, so He can speak to others through your example?

Don't let anyone look down on you because you are young, but set an example of the believers in speech, in conduct, in love, in faith and in purity. - 1 Timothy 4:12

God wants to use you as an example. He used me as an example of faith but if I had a little more wisdom and understanding, He could have used me as an example of conduct as well. Respond to the word God has spoken to you, so you can be an example to other believers in every area: how you carry yourself with grace, how you speak to others in love, how you treat people with kindness, how you remain pure throughout the process, and how you step out in faith. These are all ways God can use you as an example. Do you know that as Christians we are called to be walking epistles? Do you know we are to be examples of God's Word in human form?

"You yourselves are our letter, written on our hearts, known and read by everyone. You show that you are a letter from Christ, the result of our ministry, written not with ink but with the Spirit of the living God, not on tablets of stone but on tablets of human hearts." - 2 Corinthians 3:2-3

I want to share a story about a man in the Bible whom God also used as an example, though his situation seemed very peculiar—maybe even outlandish in his time. The prophet Hosea was instructed by God to marry a prostitute. The purpose of this was for him to be an example of God's relationship with Israel. God used Hosea's relationship with Gomer, his wife, as a means of speaking to His people. Not only that, but He gave Hosea a child as well. Their lives were examples of what God was prophetically speaking during that time.

When the Lord began to speak through Hosea, the Lord said to him, "Go, marry a promiscuous woman and have children with her, for like an adulterous wife this land is guilty of unfaithfulness to the Lord." So he married

Part I - God Speaks in Many Ways

Gomer daughter of Diblaim, and she conceived and bore him a son.

Then the Lord said to Hosea, "Call him Jezreel, because I will soon punish the house of Jehu for the massacre at Jezreel, and I will put an end to the kingdom of Israel. In that day I will break Israel's bow in the Valley of Jezreel."

Gomer conceived again and gave birth to a daughter. Then the Lord said to Hosea, "Call her Lo-Ruhamah (which means "not loved"), for I will no longer show love to Israel, that I should at all forgive them. Yet I will show love to Judah; and I will save them—not by bow, sword or battle, or by horses and horsemen, but I, the Lord their God, will save them. (Hosea 1:2-7)

Are you obedient to what God is telling you to do? Maybe He is speaking to you, so He can speak through you to others. Hearing God's voice is bigger than just you. That's why it's very important to spend time with the Lord and make sure we are hearing Him accurately and clearly. Hearing God clearly and seeking His wisdom and understanding impacts everyone positively for the glory of God. On the other hand, when we hear God inaccurately and try to perform to please people, we can lead them astray because of our bad example.

We will be held accountable for the way we live after claiming "God told me" to do this or that. Those words are very heavy; don't take them lightly. If God really told you, then your life needs to reflect His character and nature. Do not ruin your witness by operating in disorder and confusion, as well as hurting everyone you meet, even though you said God told you.

The best way that we can be examples for God is by knowing the God we want to exemplify. We are called to be ambassadors for Christ; therefore, we should represent Him everywhere we go (2 Corinthians 5:20). To truly look like Him, we must spend time in His presence and read His Word. This is how we will truly hear His voice.

Anyone who listens to the word but does not do what it says is like someone who looks at his face in a mirror and, after looking at himself, goes away and immediately forgets what he looks like.
- James 1:23-24

Don't forget what you look like beloved. Don't forget to carry God's Word inside of you wherever you go. You are an ambassador for Christ. Be an example.

Part 2

Revelatory Gifts of the Spirit

Introduction

Some believers can hear from God at a greater degree because they have certain spiritual gifts other believers may not have. You don't believe me?

Read 1 Corinthians 12:11:

> It is the one and only Spirit who distributes all these gifts. He alone decides which gift each person should have.

We can't decide what spiritual gifts we get. God gives them to us according to His will and desire. He also chooses the measure of gifts he gives to each individual. Hence, some people may have all the spiritual gifts, while some may have a few.

Still, it's important to know we can ask God for more gifts, and He will likely give them to us. For example, one of my very strong spiritual gifts is the word of knowledge. I know a lot of things simply because God reveals them to me. Yet, I lacked the wisdom to apply the knowledge I knew. So I prayed and asked the Lord for the spiritual gift, the "word of wisdom." He has faithfully given it to me because I earnestly desired it.

People ask me all the time, "How are you so wise but so young?" It's not me. It's the gift. Even more, it's the God who gave me the gift. It is not my abilities. Many of the gifts work together and complement one another. Therefore, if I feel I lack in an area, I pray to God for whatever gift I desire according to His will. The Bible encourages us to "eagerly desire spiritual gifts" (1 Corinthians 14:1). So God is not playing favoritism with those He gives spiritual gifts to. It's simply that in our weakness, He wants us to seek Him and draw closer to Him. He wants us to eagerly desire the spiritual gifts, not for the acclaim or fame, but so we can experience more of Him and bring Him glory.

Part two of this book will cover the ways you can hear God at a greater level. In part one, we talked about the ways we can hear God, which every believer has access and the ability to do. In part two, we will examine the special ways certain believers hear God even more, depending on their spiritual gifts and the desire to draw closer to Him.

CHAPTER 5

Prophetically Speaking

The gift of prophecy edifies, exhorts, and comforts (1 Corinthians 14:3). It helps us build up or strengthen and should lead us to the Word of God. The heart of prophecy is the testimony of Jesus.

A lot of people nowadays look at the prophetic as if it's something spooky, creepy or weird. This is against what we are commanded to do in the Bible. Actually, prophecy is one of the greatest spiritual gifts you can have. "Follow the way of love and eagerly desire gifts of the Spirit, especially prophecy" (1 Corinthians 14:1). The greatest fruit of the Spirit is love, but the greatest spiritual gift is the gift of prophecy. That is because when we prophesy, others are edified and uplifted.

We are commanded in 1 Thessalonians 5:19-22, "Do not quench the Spirit. Do not treat prophecies with contempt but test them all; hold on to what is good, reject every kind of evil."

Are you not encouraged when someone prophesies over you? Are you not edified and feel loved to know God has set aside a specific word and promise for you? Let's be honest; we all love to know God is thinking about us, and He would go out of His way to send someone with a word for us directly from His throne. But these days, even believers treat prophecy with contempt. They act as if they are too holy for a word from the Lord. They may say things in religious pride like, "I don't need a word from the Lord. I don't need a prophecy. I already have God's Word. I already have the Bible." Well, great! And it's probably because of that pride they will not receive a prophetic word.

"Likewise you younger people, submit yourselves to your elders. Yes, all of you be submissive to one another, and be clothed with humility, for "God resists the proud, but gives grace to the humble." - 1 Peter 5:5

God resists all forms of pride, even if we try to dress it up in religion. If there was no purpose for prophecy, if God didn't think any of us "needed" it then why would He even create the gift? Why would He appoint people as prophets? Why would He say to desire the gift of prophecy above all other gifts? God doesn't waste anything.

We have to stop trying to isolate and push away prophets in the church. We have to stop being embarrassed by our brothers and sisters in Christ who are flowing in the gift of prophecy. It's like a teenager who doesn't want his siblings around when he's hanging out with his other friends. Some of us in the church love to hang out with the world so much, we despise the parts of the body the world may not fully understand. We despise the parts of the body that don't seem dignified or glorified in the eyes of the world. However, instead of abhorring the prophetic part of the body, we should protect it.

> In fact, some parts of the body that seem weakest and least important are actually the most necessary. And the parts we regard as less honorable are those we clothe with the greatest care. So we carefully protect those parts that should not be seen, while the more honorable parts do not require this special care. So God has put the body together such that extra honor and care are given to those parts that have less dignity. (1 Corinthians 12:22-24)

We can't keep calling "crazy" what God has put in place. You can't be part Christian. You're either all in or all out. We are the body of Christ; we are one. We have to stop with the divisions.

> And he gave some, apostles; and some, prophets; and some, evangelists; and some, pastors and teachers; For the perfecting of the saints, for the work of the ministry, for the edifying of the body of Christ: Till we all come in the unity of the faith, and of the knowledge of the Son of God, unto a perfect man, unto the measure of the stature of the fullness of Christ. (Ephesians 4:11-13)

Part II - Revelatory Gifts of the Spirit

The purpose of the five-fold ministry is for the unity of the faith. We are all one body in Christ.

> *"Do not treat prophecies with contempt but test them all."*
> *- 1 Thessalonians 5:19-22*

You must know and understand what prophecy is in the first place. Prophecy is not fortune-telling. A prophet is not a psychic with a crystal ball who is using demonic spirits to tell you everything you want to hear about your future. Prophets hear directly from God; they share the word of the Lord. You must also know how to test a prophecy. If you receive a prophecy that does not bear witness with your spirit, you don't have to accept it.

> At this I fell at his feet to worship him. But he said to me, "Don't do that! I am a fellow servant with you and with your brothers and sisters who hold to the testimony of Jesus. Worship God! For it is the Spirit of prophecy who bears testimony to Jesus. (Revelation 19:10)

John bowed down to worship the angel that delivered a prophetic word to him. However, the angel rebuked Him. We are not called to worship prophets or the prophecy. Rather, we are to worship God alone. This angel was only a messenger of God. Likewise, anyone sent with a prophetic word is only a messenger delivering the word of the Lord to the people.

I once heard a minister say, "A prophet is simply a glorified parrot." In other words, you are just a vessel repeating the word given by the Lord. According to this scripture, the spirit of prophecy is the testimony of Jesus. So if you receive a so-called "prophetic word," but it in no way reflects the testimony of Jesus, then it may not be the spirit of prophecy.

We must test the spirit behind that prophetic word. It must be birthed out of the testimony of Jesus. The first step is to test the word but the next step is to test the spirit behind that word. How do you test the spirit?

> Dear friends, do not believe everyone who claims to speak by the Spirit. You must test them to see if the spirit they have comes from God. For there are many false prophets in the world. This is how we know if they have the Spirit of God: If a person claiming to be a prophet acknowledges that Jesus Christ came in a real body, that person has the Spirit of God. But if someone claims to be a prophet and does not acknowledge the truth about Jesus, that person is not from God. Such a person has the spirit of the Antichrist, which you heard is coming into the world and indeed is already here. (1 John 4:1-3)

When you receive a prophecy from someone, and it doesn't sit well with your spirit, ask that person, "Has Jesus Christ come in the flesh?" This prophecy must bear witness with you. If it doesn't, then you should always test it. Not only should we test the spirits, but we should also know that God is testing us.

> Suppose there are prophets among you or those who dream dreams about the future, and they promise you signs or miracles, and the predicted signs or miracles occur. If they then say, 'Come, let us worship other gods'—gods you have not known before— do not listen to them. The Lord your **God is testing you** to see if you truly love him with all your heart and soul. (Deuteronomy 13:1-3)

God is testing all of us. He wants to know if we truly love Him with all our hearts and souls or if we just love what He can give us. Are you more focused on chasing down the promise or prophetic word that you've received than you are about following Christ? Will you deny God and take up the idols you feel meet your desires, especially if you believe God is taking too long to come through or answer your prayers? Will you abandon God when you get frustrated? Will you turn to other gods?

Remember 1 Thessalonians 5:19 says: "Do not quench the spirit." When we live in sin, we reject the voice of the Holy Spirit and silence Him from speaking to us. We should not treat prophecies with contempt. When you feed your flesh, it is loud. When you starve your Spirit, you quench it. So if you have been living in the flesh, maybe you're not hearing God.

Perhaps you only hear your flesh. Maybe you're just following your deceitful heart.

"The heart is deceitful above all things and beyond cure. Who can understand it?" - Jeremiah 17:9

You can't hear the Holy Spirit clearly if you are constantly living in the flesh. When was the last time you fasted and prayed? When was the last time you denied your flesh to build up your spirit man? To prophesy or hear God clearly concerning what's to come, you must have God's Word hidden in your heart. Otherwise, you will sin against Him. Your flesh will take the lead.

"Direct my footsteps according to your word; let no sin rule over me." - Psalm 119:133

We are led by God. He directs the footsteps of our lives according to His Word. Without His Word, we have no direction. I also love the verse in Psalm 119:105, which says, "Your word is a lamp to my feet and a light to my path." Is God's Word leading you? Or is your flesh leading you? The heart of prophecy is the testimony of Jesus. If you don't have the testimony of Jesus in your heart, if you don't have God's Word inside of you, how can you hear God? How can you prophesy?

Therefore, carry God's Word in your heart and spend time with Him. Don't treat prophecies with contempt; instead, eagerly desire this spiritual gift. God wants to speak to you. He wants to share His secrets with you and use you as a vessel to edify the body of Christ. Are you willing to be trained in this spiritual gift?

CHAPTER 6

Tongues & Interpretation

When we are saved and born again, we are all marked with a special seal confirming our salvation. This seal is the Holy Spirit according to Ephesians 1:13. The baptism of the Holy Spirit is a beautiful rebirth for the believer. Through water baptism, we make a public declaration that we have put on the new man and put away the old man of sin. It is a sign we have been reborn. Yet, through the fire baptism of the Holy Spirit, we don't just put on the new man; we put on the spirit man.

The Spirit of the living God is inside of us, working in and through us. Jesus Himself promises in John 16:13: "When the Spirit of truth comes, he will guide you into all truth. He will not speak on his own but will tell you what he has heard. He will tell you about the future." Isn't that beautiful? In the early church, men could only hear from God by external means but today, we can hear God from within. We can hear from God for ourselves and have a personal relationship with Him. We don't need a high priest to go to God on our behalf; we are all priests.

When Jesus died, the veil was torn, and He went to be with the Father. The veil was a symbol of the law. It was used in the tabernacle to separate the Holies of Holies from the Holy Place. Now, since the veil has been torn, we don't have to be separate from God, though He is holy. We are the righteousness of God in Christ (2 Corinthians 5:21). We are now seated in high places with Christ Jesus (Ephesians 2:6). We are in heavenly places and because of the Holy Spirit, we have a heavenly language given by a holy God. It all started on the day of Pentecost as recorded in the book of Acts.

"They saw what seemed to be tongues of fire that separated and came to rest on each of them. All of them were filled with the Holy Spirit and began to speak in other tongues as the Spirit enabled them." - Acts 2:3-4

Your relationship with God is taken to a new level when you have the baptism of the Holy Spirit. Before I received the baptism of the Holy Spirit, I could only hear God by reading His Word but even then it was hard for me to understand what it all really meant. After receiving the baptism of the Holy Spirit and the ability to speak in tongues, I realized my Bible study time went to a whole new level.

The Holy Spirit began speaking to me from within, and I could receive the rhema word. Before, I only had the logos word. The purpose of speaking in tongues is for the believer to be edified individually. This is made clear in the Bible, which says, "Anyone who speaks in a tongue edifies themselves, but the one who prophesies edifies the church" (1 Corinthians 14:4).

Speaking in tongues helped me to grow in my walk with God and understanding His Word. You will hear God speaking to you as you edify yourself.

Every born again believer has the Holy Spirit living on the inside and can speak in tongues, our heavenly prayer language. Our prayer language cannot be known or interpreted.

> For if you have the ability to speak in tongues, you will be talking only to God, since people won't be able to understand you. You will be speaking by the power of the Spirit, but it will all be mysterious. (1 Corinthians 14:2)

Let me clarify this even further because many people become confused at this point. Our heavenly language or our prayer language as some may call it cannot be understood because it is only between us and God. We can't even understand it but the Holy Spirit makes groanings and intercessions on our behalf. God is praying for us when we speak in our heavenly language; He is not speaking to us. We are being edified because as we are speaking in tongues, God is praying. As a result, we are being built up, strengthened, and encouraged.

> In the same way, the Spirit helps us in our weakness. We do not know what we ought to pray for, but the Spirit himself intercedes for us through wordless groans. And he who searches our hearts knows the mind of the Spirit, because

the Spirit intercedes for God's people in accordance with the will of God. (Romans 8:26-27)

There is a spiritual gift or another kind of tongues people tend to confuse with our heavenly language. This spiritual gift is called "diverse tongues," which can be interpreted and known. It is the "tongues of man," rather than the "heavenly tongues." All believers can speak in tongues, which is their heavenly language. However, not all believers have the spiritual gift of speaking in diverse tongues. When believers are operating in this spiritual gift, God is not praying for them. Rather, God is using them to speak to others. Therefore, the tongues *must* be interpreted. Interpretation is also a spiritual gift. When you have the gift of diverse tongues or interpretation, you can hear from God in a unique way that the average believer does not.

Now, I want to go deeper into defining these manifestation gifts of the Holy Spirit.

1. **Diverse tongues** - Supernatural utterances through the power of the Holy Spirit in a person that manifests as spiritual language. Involving the ability to speak in a foreign language(s) not previously studied.

2. **Interpretation** - A supernatural verbalization and subsequent interpretation of the diverse tongue. This gift operates out of the mind of the Spirit rather than out of the mind of man.

I've heard stories of people speaking in languages they didn't know how to speak. For example, someone who only speaks English can be used by the Holy Spirit to manifest a diverse tongue of speaking in Spanish or another foreign language that a group of people can understand. That group of people is not operating in the gift of interpretation if the tongue manifested by the speaker is a language they already know and understand. Rather, the one who interprets should not have any prior knowledge or understanding of the spiritual tongue. The Holy Spirit gives them divine revelation to interpret what it actually means and what the Spirit of the Lord is saying.

This is how the church should operate to maintain order. All of us must function in our spiritual giftings. I love that I attend a Spirit-filled church where every now and then, the power of God manifests in someone declaring a diverse tongue. Following that, another member of our church is naturally prompted by the Holy Spirit to interpret it. This is a way God will use two people in the body of Christ through their spiritual gifts to speak to the larger group or body. Together, we are all edified. This is how the church of God should operate.

"If anyone speaks in a tongue, two--or at the most three--should speak, one at a time, and someone must interpret. If there is no interpreter, the speaker should keep quiet in the church and speak to himself and to God." - 1 Corinthians 14:27-28

If you often burst out in tongues in the middle of church and there is no one there to interpret, maybe you are simply speaking in your heavenly prayer language, not a diverse tongue. If no one understands what you are saying, they weren't meant to. Meaning, it's supposed to be a secret and intimate moment between you and the Lord.

Your prayer time is supposed to be private. It is not exposed to everyone so you can appear holy. Your prayer language is not meant to be displayed on blast. Don't worry; I've made this same mistake in the past as well. But if God decides to use you to speak in a diverse tongue during a church meeting or assembly, trust that He will also use someone else who is there to interpret.

"When you pray, don't be like the hypocrites who love to pray publicly on street corners and in the synagogues where everyone can see them. I tell you the truth, that is all the reward they will ever get." - Matthew 6:5

As I mentioned in the introduction, many of these gifts complement one another. Some people have the gift of diverse tongues, as well as interpretation. In their private time, they may speak in a diverse tongue, though they may think it is their prayer language. Then, God gives them the interpretation of what they just said; that is a diverse tongue. This has happened only a few times in my life. Most of the time when I am speaking in tongues, I have no idea what I am saying. But there have been a few times when God gives me a full interpretation, and I understand what He is saying to me. In that moment, I am not only edified, but I also receive divine instruction and hear from God at the same time. How precious are God's spiritual gifts to us? They are such blessings!

I love that we all have different gifts in the body of Christ. With the gifts God has given me, I get to serve the body of Christ and enjoy the gifts of others. God doesn't use me for everything, but when He does use me, I am grateful, honored, and content. When God uses the gifts of others, such a prophecy, diverse tongues, and interpretation, I am truly blessed. I love when He speaks to me in these ways.

CHAPTER 7

Word of Knowledge

Word of Knowledge — A definite conviction, impression or knowing that comes to you in a mental picture, dream, vision, or a scripture that is quickened to you.

One of my spiritual gifts is the "word of knowledge." Through this spiritual gift, God reveals things to me I wouldn't have otherwise known. Word of knowledge is not "common knowledge." One would expect the average person to have common knowledge and understanding of the basic universal principles and widely accepted facts. For example, knowing that the sky is blue is not the word of knowledge; it's common knowledge. Word of knowledge comes directly from the Holy Spirit. It is not something that is widely or easily known. It is something He reveals to you.

This gift is often used in ministry when God is trying to teach you a little more about someone else. When ministering healing and deliverance to others, sometimes the only way we can address those deep and hidden wounds is to receive a word of knowledge about that person's past or current situation. For example, the word of knowledge might be something like, "This person was abused as a child" or "This man is struggling with pornography addiction." In this case, it is nothing that you guess, discern or assume. It is simply a word of knowledge quickened in your spirit from the Lord.

This spiritual gift takes a lot of responsibility. God has to be able to trust you with the secrets of others if you desire Him to speak to you in this way. When you are given a word of knowledge about others, it is most often to serve them. You can pray more specific prayers for them. You can speed up the healing and deliverance process for them by getting to the root of the issue, rather than trying to dig or beat around the bush. Be careful not to shame or judge others when you know their secrets. That is not the purpose of this spiritual gift.

I can recall one time when God gave me a word of knowledge about a young lady. He revealed to me she was struggling with masturbation behind closed doors. I didn't mention anything to her about it until she confessed this struggle to me that same day. The word of knowledge God gave me about her was used to convict her in a loving way. She felt exposed but not to the point of embarrassment. Because of her confession, I was able to pray with her and stand in agreement for her healing and deliverance in this area.

> *"Therefore confess your sins to each other and pray for each other so that you may be healed. The prayer of a righteous person is powerful and effective." - James 5:16*

The word of knowledge can be used in practical cases as well, not just in ministry. In my life, I have experienced this gift in regards to my relationships, business plans, and even my travel plans. For example, before I leave the house, God might say, "There's a huge accident on I-4. Take another route." I'll listen to the radio and sure enough, there will be an accident just as it was spoken to me.

As you can see, this spiritual gift will give you an advantage in hearing God's voice. It is also very specific. The word of knowledge can be used to help you make the right decision, protect you from harm, and minister to others. People will ask you, "How did you know?" But it is not because you are a psychic. You simply know because God has given you supernatural knowledge through this revelatory gift.

CHAPTER 8

Word of Wisdom

The word of knowledge and word of wisdom work hand in hand. As do many other spiritual gifts, they complement one another. For the longest while, I was operating in the word of knowledge. However, I felt I lacked the wisdom to apply the knowledge God had given me. Now, this leads me to the definition of this spiritual gift:

Word of Wisdom: Application of the knowledge God gives you. Seeing life from God's perspective.

We must receive wisdom from the Lord to grow in understanding and apply His instructions to our lives. If we are honest, we would admit we are frustrated, and it's not because we don't hear from God. It's because we don't have the wisdom to carry out what God is telling us to do. We are afraid, confused, and uncertain which step to take next. Slow down, seek the face of God, and He will give you the wisdom you need. If God told you to do something, now is the time to labor over it in prayer.

Part II - Revelatory Gifts of the Spirit

As mentioned previously, in 2015, I received a word from God to leave my college university. Though I believe I heard God clearly, I wish I would have asked Him for the wisdom to go about that transition. I probably could have handled things better and saved a lot of money, but I didn't truly understand what God wanted me to do. Still, I was obedient, even though I didn't fully understand. I looked crazy to my family, friends, and schoolmates. But maybe I didn't have to look so crazy if I had just gone to the Lord for wisdom.

God may be speaking to you. He may be calling you to step out in faith. He may be leading you to leave your job or move to another country. Please, don't neglect using wisdom. I know you're excited. I know you're passionate about serving the Lord, and you have the gift of faith. You could ruin your witness if you rush into something declaring, "God said," but you don't have the wisdom and understanding to gracefully carry out His instructions. Maybe God did say to do this or that, and I know you might be very excited to start this new venture, but don't be so focused on starting that you're not prepared to finish. Count the cost.

"But don't begin until you count the cost. For who would begin construction of a building without first calculating the cost to see if there is enough money to finish it?" - Luke 14:28

One of the biggest lessons I have learned about hearing God's voice and receiving instruction from the Lord is that I need to be a faithful steward of the word He has given me. His word is a seed and if I plant, protect, and nourish it properly, it will grow and bear much fruit. Many of us take the word God has spoken to us, but it doesn't flourish because we lack wisdom. We don't know how to plant that the word, so it manifests in our lives.

God has given you a big vision but are you protecting it? Or do you go on social media and share your vision for the whole world to see? Be careful about sharing your plans with others. Believe it or not, not everyone is happy for you and some people will pray for your demise. Others may try to discourage you, uproot the seed God has planted in your heart, try to steal the vision or build it on their own. How are you stewarding the word God has spoken to you?

Are you taking care of your vision by carefully planning it out with the help of the Holy Spirit? God has given some people business ideas, but they are not even faithful enough to write out the business plan. God has given others instructions to write a book, but they won't even jot down the outline. What is God telling you to do? Habakkuk 2:2 says, "Then the LORD answered me and said: 'Write the vision and make it plain on tablets, that he may run who reads it.'"

How can you run forth with the word God has given you if you can't even write down the vision and make it plain? To make it "plain" means to make it clear and understandable. Some of you are unable to run with the word God has spoken to you because you are still confused about exactly what to do. You lack wisdom and understanding on how to carry it out. Writing down the vision can bring clarity and understanding; it will help you to create a plan.

Part II - Revelatory Gifts of the Spirit

"The plans of the diligent lead surely to abundance, but everyone who is hasty comes only to poverty."
- Proverbs 21:5

Create a plan with the help of the Holy Spirit. He will direct your path. The plans God gives you will not always make sense to you but trust Him because they are good. "'For I know the plans I have for you,' declares the Lord, 'plans to prosper you and not to harm you, plans to give you hope and a future'" (Jeremiah 29:11). Ask God what the plan is. Ask Him for understanding and wisdom.

We shouldn't have to rely on our own understanding nor should we desire to. Don't build your tower or vision with man's wisdom or a worldly understanding but with spiritual wisdom and God's divine instruction. Don't rely on what you can see because we walk by faith, not by sight (2 Corinthians 5:7). We must be surrendered to the Lord in prayer. We must spend more time in His presence.

"Trust in the Lord with all your heart and lean not on your own understanding; in all your ways submit to him, and he will make your paths straight." - Proverbs 3:5-6

It is not enough for you to spend 10% of your time with God, receive a word, and try to carry out that word in 90% of your time. You will make a lot of mistakes and get burned out because you are spending more time performing than hearing from God. If we want to pour out, we must be poured into first. We should spend 90% of our time hearing from the Lord, spending time with Him, receiving His wisdom, guidance, and plan. In doing so, we will be more successful in the 10% of performing than we could ever be with the 90% when we were barely spending time with Him.

If God gives you a word of knowledge about someone else, especially if the word is very personal and touches a sensitive topic, approach the matter carefully. You need God's wisdom to deal with that word of knowledge in a way that protects the hearts of everyone involved. The same could also go for the gift of prophecy. You may receive a prophetic word. However, don't rush to share it. Allow God to give you the wisdom to deliver that prophetic word. Is it a word for now? Is it a word for later? Should it be delivered over the phone or in person? Should you speak with a gentle or firm tone? These differences really matter. Only with God's wisdom and guidance can you deliver a prophetic word in the exact way He desires.

Wisdom is needed in every area of our lives, not just when it comes to operating in spiritual gifts. The voice of wisdom will guide us in the right way if we listen. The spiritual gift, the word of wisdom allows us to see life from God's perspective. The only way we can do that is to fear Him and view life through the lens of His Word. God's Word is a mirror of His perspective. Wisdom is calling out. Are you listening?

"Wisdom calls aloud outside; she raises her voice in the open squares. She cries out in the chief concourses, at the openings of the gates in the city she speaks her words." - Proverbs 1:20-21

Wisdom is not silent. She is very loud. But we must listen. If we don't fear the Lord, our hearts are hardened and our ears and eyes are made dull. :

"Then they will call on me, but I will not answer; they will seek me diligently, but they will not find me because they hated knowledge and did not choose the fear of the Lord."
- Proverbs 1:28-29

God seems quiet to some of us because we do not fear Him. We've despised knowledge. We do not hear the loud cry of wisdom though we are on our faces in prayer. That happens because we refuse to accept God's discipline and learn when He rebukes us. God disciplines those whom He loves according to Hebrews 12:6. When God tells you not to do something, and you are disobedient time and time again, you quench the voice of the Holy Spirit. You grieve God's Spirit. Hence, you can't hear Him as you used to. Do you fear God? Were you obedient to the last thing He told you to do? Obedience is where it starts.

"The fear of the LORD is the beginning of wisdom, and knowledge of the Holy One is understanding." - Proverbs 9:10

We must have wisdom, knowledge, and understanding. These all go hand in hand and bring another element of depth to our walk with God. So before dropping everything and moving to a different state or leaving your fulltime job to go into ministry, seek God's wisdom on how to carry out what you know about your future and what He told you. Look into the mirror of His Word to be reminded of God's perspective on how to do things. You want to make sure you are seeing life from His viewpoint. Do not harden your heart or run away in fear or disobedience. Instead, run into your prayer closet and wait on clear instruction from the Lord.

CHAPTER 9

Visions and Dreams

God can speak to us in dreams, as well as open visions. Acts 2:17 says, "'In the last days,' God says, 'I will pour out my Spirit upon all people. Your sons and daughters will prophesy. Your young men will see visions, and your old men will dream dreams." In one instance, I had an open vision (vision while awake) that my car was spinning on the highway. Shortly after, I got into a car accident (thankfully God protected me); the car spun off the road. It was exactly as I saw it in the vision, and it came to pass that same day. The open vision was a form of communication God used to speak to me.

I am a dreamer and have multiple—at least, three dreams on a nightly basis. I even had a dream of going to heaven once. I have seen many of my visions and dreams come to pass whether in the natural or spiritual. I learned that God can give us visions and dreams as a way of speaking to us. He also spoke to many men in the Bible this way.

In the book of Daniel, King Nebuchadnezzar had a troubling dream, which Daniel, God's servant, was able to interpret. "During the night the mystery was revealed to Daniel in a vision. Then Daniel praised the God of heaven" (Daniel 2:19). The dream prophetically spoke of the future of the kingdoms that were to arise. God used Daniel as a vessel to speak to King Nebuchadnezzar and declare the destiny of the nation of Israel.

In Genesis Chapter 41, God sent Pharaoh a dream and Joseph interpreted it. Through this dream, Joseph's interpretation, and godly wisdom, a successful strategy was implemented for the nation to survive a 7-year famine. In the previous examples, God sent dreams and interpreters to speak prophetically to the nations. In the same way, God can personally send dreams to speak prophetically to you.

God sends us dreams for several reasons. They can be prophetic messages, warnings, confirmations, revelations or ideas. I've realized all the revelatory spiritual gifts such as prophecy, the word of wisdom, the word of knowledge, etc. all tend to manifest in visions and dreams. For example, I've heard of people who received ideas for businesses, inventions, and books through their visions and dreams. Breakthroughs to medicine, solutions for broken relationships, warnings about people with ulterior motives, and confirmations of future plans are all beautiful revelations God can give us through visions and dreams.

Now that we have gone over the beauty and benefits of receiving visions and dreams, it's important to know the dark side. We are warned in 1 Peter 5:8, "Stay alert! Watch out for your great enemy, the devil. He prowls around like a roaring lion, looking for someone to devour." Our adversary is a counterfeit who tries to copy everything God does in a perverted way. So he can give us dreams too. He tries to get us to fall into sin, sexual perversion or confusion through our dreams. He may give us nightmares, lustful dreams or false visions and ideas that bring confusion and strife into our lives. Therefore, it's very important to pray and anoint yourself before you sleep. Recognize that not every dream is from God.

Just because you have a dream from God, it doesn't make it a confirmation. Maybe the dream wasn't from God. So what is the first thing you do when you get one of these dreams? Do you pray about it? Or do you run to the Internet or your friends? The best interpreter of your dreams is the Holy Spirit, not your friends or any online search engine.

It's also a waste of time seeking dream interpretations without knowing the source of the dream. If the dream isn't from God, we shouldn't care for an interpretation. Dreams from false sources can only lend to false interpretations that add no value to our lives. That is why the first thing we should do is pray. When we pray, before asking God for the dream's interpretation out of anxiety to receive a confirmation, we should ask God if the dream is even from Him. Many times, we should be able to discern if it is or not.

If you always take your dreams to everyone else without ever consulting God, you're setting yourself up for deception. The Enemy can use that opportunity to send false prophets into your life to "interpret" the dream he may have given you himself. Alternatively, he may twist the dream God gave you out of context.

"For the household gods utter nonsense, and the diviners see lies; they tell false dreams and give empty consolation. Therefore the people wander like sheep; They are afflicted for lack of a shepherd." - Zechariah 10:2

Are you spending enough time with Jesus to know His voice and follow Him? If you are, you will be more comfortable and confident going to Him about your dream than to everyone else. Or do you spend more time with your friends listening to their opinions? Are they your gods?

Examine your dream. What sticks out? Does anything in it represent a symbol or theme presented within or throughout the Bible? You must be familiar with God's Word to know those references, signs, symbols, and metaphors for yourself. The first book we should be running to when we have moments like this is not some "Book of Dreams" written by a man or woman. Rather, we should go to the Bible and our prayer closet. I understand many of us have gone to the wrong sources. I have, too, so I'm preaching to myself! But we should run to God Himself.

Why aren't we willing to put a little extra time and effort into discovering what the Holy Spirit wants to show us for ourselves? Some of us are lazy and demanding at the same time. "Now, now, now, God! I want to know the interpretation now but I'm so anxious. I don't have time to pray. I don't have time to sit before your feet in silence. I don't have time to go to the Word. I will have my answer before you know it if I just type "Dream Symbols" in an online search!" Sometimes we trust and depend on the Internet more than we do the Holy Spirit. That should not be.

Your dream may even be from you. I minored in psychology when I went to school and I was able to take a class on dreams and sleep. Granted, I don't believe psychology is the answer or explanation to everything and sometimes things are simply spiritual. Nevertheless, at the same time, some truths can be found in psychology, and it does play a role.

I learned in class it is very likely for us to dream about anything we're obsessing over during the day or triggers we may pick up throughout the day because they remain in our subconscious. In spiritual terms, I would translate it as, the manifestation of a seed being planted in your heart. That seed may be a thought you had, a movie you watched, a conversation you engaged in, which became a trigger and open door for the dream.

I don't want to sound harsh, but I have to be real with you. We must recognize the triggers and open doors we create in our lives. If we go through life blaming God, the Devil, and everyone else without truly evaluating our actions and taking responsibility, we will live in confusion. We will always think we're right and everyone else is wrong.

Guard your heart in this season from what you say, think, and watch. Ultimately, what you put in front and inside of you will determine your path. We want to make sure we're putting God's Word in front of us, that sincere prayer and praise are constantly flowing out of us, and the Holy Spirit is dwelling in us. Not junk.

"Above all else, guard your heart, for everything you do flows from it." - Proverbs 4:23

    When you are guarding your heart, reading God's Word, and spending time in God's presence that is the best way you can hear Him accurately. The more time you spend with Him, the more you will recognize His voice overtime.

CHAPTER 10

Why Is God Silent?

We may feel God isn't speaking at some points in our lives because we are going through a test. When this happens, we should remember God has already spoken. He has trained, taught, and prepared you for this moment. As the saying goes, "The teacher doesn't speak during the test."

Whenever we first get saved, we tend to feel as if we are very close to God. We are excited and on fire for God. We are always reading the Word and getting new revelations about life. Our eyes are opened and God is teaching us many new things. Then, for some reason, the fire seems to fizzle.

I encourage you to keep that fire burning. Keep that lamp lit until Christ's return. It may seem hard to wait on God sometimes, but we have such great hope to cling on to. Matthew Chapter 25 tells of the ten virgins with the lamps; five of them were foolish and five were wise.

> The foolish ones took their lamps but did not take any oil with them. The wise ones, however, took oil in jars along with their lamps. The

bridegroom was a long time in coming, and they all became drowsy and fell asleep. (Matthew 25:3-5)

Beloved, don't become drowsy and fall asleep. The oil is produced when you spend time with God. Even if you feel you're in a silent season, have confidence in knowing God is still with you. He has not left you. If you don't feel He's speaking to you, continue to seek Him with due diligence. Ask Him to break any hardness of heart that may be blocking you from receiving His wisdom. If you haven't done so already, be obedient and carry out the last instruction He told you to do. The test has begun; will you pass it?

What are you doing with everything God taught you in the last season? Did you just forget about it? You are in the test right now, and God is not going to baby you anymore. Maybe He wants to teach you about patience, waiting on Him, and seeking Him more. Maybe He wants to teach you about contentment, keeping your eyes on Christ, and off of this world. Perhaps He is teaching you about having faith, as well as enduring and persevering throughout the process. He wants you to apply all everything you've learned and pass the test in *this* season. Remember, He has spoken. He is speaking, and He will continue to speak. Have you been listening? What did He tell you?

Made in the USA
Monee, IL
14 April 2022